Challenge

Level K

Blackline Masters

A Division of The McGraw-Hill Companies

Columbus, Ohio

www.sra4kids.com

SRA/McGraw-Hill

*A Division of The **McGraw·Hill** Companies*

Send all inquiries to:
SRA/McGraw-Hill
8787 Orion Place
Columbus, OH 43240-4027

Printed in the United States of America.

ISBN 0-07-572057-4

2 3 4 5 6 7 8 9 QPD 07 06 05 04 03 02

Table of Contents

GRAMMAR AND USAGE

▶ Words That Name: People and Animals

Directions: Listen as I read each word that names a person or an animal. Look at the pictures. Draw a line from the word to the picture it matches.

1. girl

2. bug

3. fox

4. man

▶ Words That Name: Objects

1. ring

2. tie

3. book

4. coat

GRAMMAR AND USAGE

▶ Words That Name: Places

GRAMMAR AND USAGE

1. road

2. home

3. zoo

4. beach

▶ Letter Recognition

SOUNDS AND LETTERS

UNIT 1 School • **Lesson 14** *Fine Art*

SOUNDS AND LETTERS

▶ Letter Recognition

Directions: Write the small letter for each capital letter.

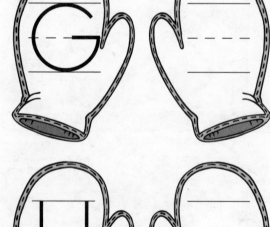

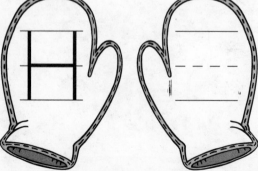

Letter Recognition • **Challenge**

UNIT 1   School • **Lesson 16** *Annabelle Swift, Kindergartner*

▶Letter Recognition

K   h   k   f   b

H   d   j   h   f

SOUNDS AND LETTERS

Challenge • *Letter Recognition*

▶Review

Directions: Listen as I read each word that names a person, an animal, an object, or a place. Look at the pictures. Draw a line from the word to the picture it matches.

GRAMMAR AND USAGE

1. queen

2. zoo

3. fork

4. duck

►Letter Recognition

B

I

H

g

D

h

G

b

L

e

E

d

SOUNDS AND LETTERS

▶ Letters to Words

WRITER'S CRAFT

Directions: Use the letters to spell a word.

1. o g   _____

2. e m   _____

3. o t   _____

4. o y u   _____

5. t i   _____

Letters to Words • Challenge

▶ Alphabetical Order

Directions: Draw a line connecting the capital letters in order from *A* to *L* to help the dog find its way home.

SOUNDS AND LETTERS

	A	B	C	D	E	F
A			K			G
C			K			H
L			K			I
F	C	J	🏠	L	K	J
M			N			D
E			O			L
B			P			B
K	G	C	D	I	F	H

GRAMMAR AND USAGE

▶ # Sentence Types: Statements and Questions

Directions: Listen as I read each sentence. Circle the sentence type I read.

1. I read the blue book. Where is your book?

2. I am six years old. How old are you?

3. When is lunch? We eat at noon.

4. Do you have a pet? I have a turtle.

▶ Words to Sentences

1. I like to read _____.   books   bananas

2. I have a pet _____.   sink   dog

3. Ice is _____.   soft   cold

4. The sun is _____.   hot   blue

FORMING LETTERS

▶ Letter Formation

Directions: Circle the capital and small forms of the letters *Ll*, *Mm*, and *Nn*.

C m d H I l l

N A c L D e

E a n l F M

f h A m G B

M b k N i j

I K J I L A

Letter Formation • **Challenge**

SOUNDS AND LETTERS

Name _____ Date _____

▶ Alphabetical Order

Directions: Connect the dots in order from *A* to *R* to complete the picture of the sailboat.

O

P•   •N

Q• •

•M

R•————————J•   K•   L•

B•   A•———I•   •H   •G

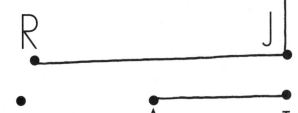   •C   •D   •E   •F

SOUNDS AND LETTERS

▶Capital Letters

Directions: Listen as I read the words. Look at the words carefully. Circle the word that uses a capital letter.

MECHANICS

1. Paul   paul

2. i   I

3. margo   Margo

4. we   We

5. The   the

6. you   You

Capital Letters • Challenge

▶Sounds and Letters

UNIT 2 Shadows • **Lesson II** *The Wolf and His Shadow*

▶End Marks

MECHANICS

Directions: Listen as I read each sentence. Circle the correct end mark.

1. Where are you   .   ?

2. Red is my favorite color   .   ?

3. Her shoes were dirty   .   ?

4. Are you my teacher   .   ?

UNIT 2 Shadows • **Lesson 12** *The Wolf and His Shadow*

▶ Sounds and Letters

T	t	T
h	L	K
F	R	j

E	R	V
d	r	n
a	R	a

v	D	R
u	V	A
n	I	v

q	b	p
Q	g	d
q	G	C

M	h	N
I	N	m
n	H	i

Challenge • *Sounds and Letters*

▶Sounds and Letters

Directions: Draw a line from each capital letter to its matching small letter.

Copyright © SRA/McGraw-Hill. Permission is granted to reproduce this page for classroom use.

SOUNDS AND LETTERS

UNIT 2 Shadows • **Lesson 14** *The Wolf and His Shadow*

▶Telling in Time Order

First, I woke up. Next, I ate breakfast.

WRITER'S CRAFT

▶Review

GRAMMAR AND USAGE

Directions: Listen as I read each sentence. Circle the correct sentence.

1. the horse jumped   The horse jumped.

2. Where is the phone?   where is the Phone

3. did you practice   Did you practice?

4. The room is small.   the room is small?

Name _____ Date _____

▶ Alphabetical Order

Directions: Draw a line connecting the small letters in order from a to z.

Copyright © SRA/McGraw-Hill. Permission is granted to reproduce this page for classroom use.

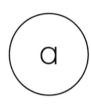  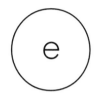 

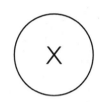 d f

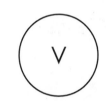 r  h

    i

   s t

 q v u h

  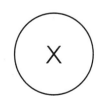  z

SOUNDS AND LETTERS

UNIT 3 Finding Friends • **Lesson 1** *Unit Introduction*

▶ Words That Describe: Color

GRAMMAR AND USAGE

1. green

2. yellow

3. brown

4. orange

Words That Describe: Color • **Challenge**

UNIT 3 Finding Friends • **Lesson I** *Unit Introduction*

▶Organizing and Collecting Data

Directions: Listen as I read the list of words that name animals. Put an X over the words that do not name an animal.

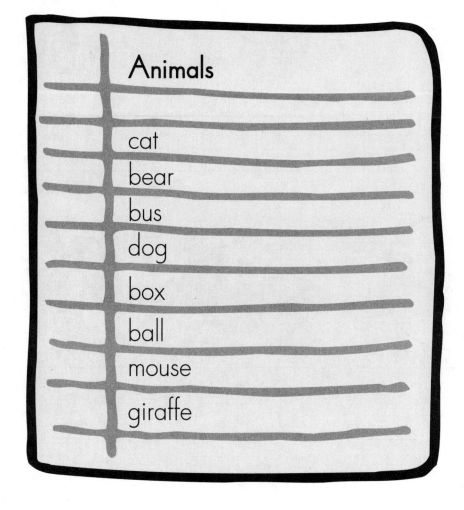

Animals

cat
bear
bus
dog
box
ball
mouse
giraffe

WRITER'S CRAFT

UNIT 3 Finding Friends • **Lesson 4** *Ginger*

▶ Phonics Skills

Directions: Write the letter that each picture begins with.

SOUNDS AND LETTERS

_____

- - - - - - - - - -

_____

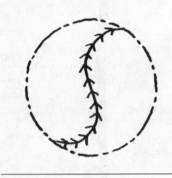

_____

- - - - - - - - - -

_____

_____

_____

_____

Phonics Skills • Challenge

▶Words That Describe: How Many

Directions: Listen to the words that describe how many that I read and look at the number. Draw a line from the number to the picture it matches.

two   2

one   1

five   5

three   3

GRAMMAR AND USAGE

UNIT 3 Finding Friends • **Lesson 6** *The Lonely Prince*

▶ Messages

Directions: Listen as I read the word or group of words. Circle the message.

WRITER'S CRAFT

1. Mom, we went for a walk.
   walk

2. Your Uncle Max called.
   phone

3. Please wash the car.
   water

4. Great work!
   paper

Messages • Challenge

UNIT 3 Finding Friends • **Lesson 9** *The Lonely Prince*

▶Phonics Skills

Directions: Find the word that names each picture. Write each word on the line below the correct picture.

| fan | bibs | ham | bat | pins |

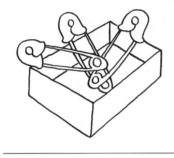

_____

- - - - - - - - - - -

_____

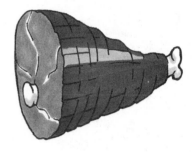

_____

- - - - - - - - - - -

_____

_____

- - - - - - - - - - -

_____

_____

- - - - - - - - - - -

_____

SOUNDS AND LETTERS

UNIT 3 **Finding Friends • Lesson II** *Making Friends*

▶ Words That Describe: Weather

GRAMMAR AND USAGE

I. rainy

2. sunny

3. snowy

Words That Describe: Weather • **Challenge**

▶ Phonics Skills

be_____

ma_____

ban_____

mo_____

po_____

SOUNDS AND LETTERS

UNIT 3   Finding Friends • **Lesson 16** *Don't Need Friends*

▶Review

Directions: Listen as I read the words that describe. Draw a picture that matches each word.

GRAMMAR AND USAGE

1. purple

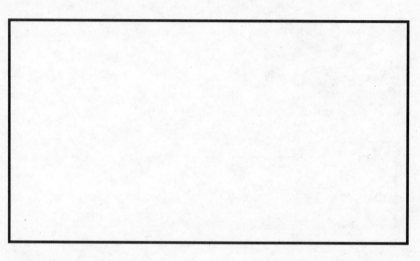

2. four

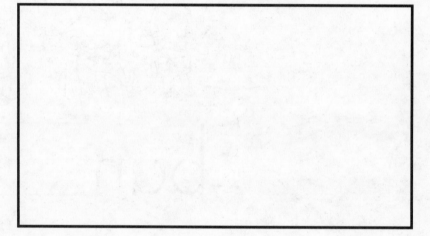

3. rainy

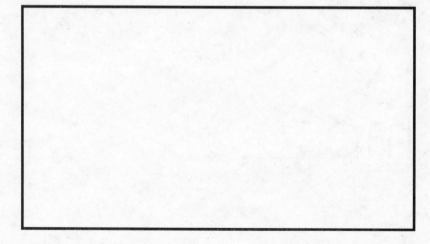

▶ Phonics Skills

i

m____p

e

p____ns

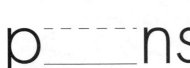

a

d____nt

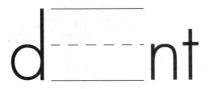

o

p____t

SOUNDS AND LETTERS

▶ Exploring Sounds and Letters

SOUNDS AND LETTERS

▶ Words That Describe: Senses

1. small

2. loud

3. white

4. hot

GRAMMAR AND USAGE

▶ Sounds and Letters

SOUNDS AND LETTERS

Sounds and Letters • Challenge

▶ Sounds and Letters

Directions: Draw a line from the letters *Mm* to each picture whose name begins with /m/.

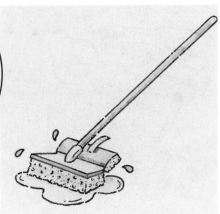

SOUNDS AND LETTERS

▶Sounds and Letters

SOUNDS AND LETTERS

Mm

Sounds and Letters • Challenge

UNIT 4   **The Wind • Lesson 6**   *What Happens When Wind Blows?*

►Sounds and Letters

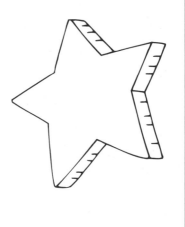

SOUNDS AND LETTERS

▶ Words That Describe: Position

1. on

2. behind

3. in

4. between

▶ Sounds and Letters

Directions: Draw a line from the letters *Dd* to each picture whose name begins with /d/.

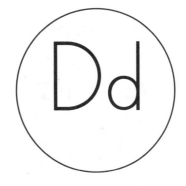

Dd

SOUNDS AND LETTERS

▶ Sounds and Letters

Directions: Color each picture whose name ends with /d/.

SOUNDS AND LETTERS

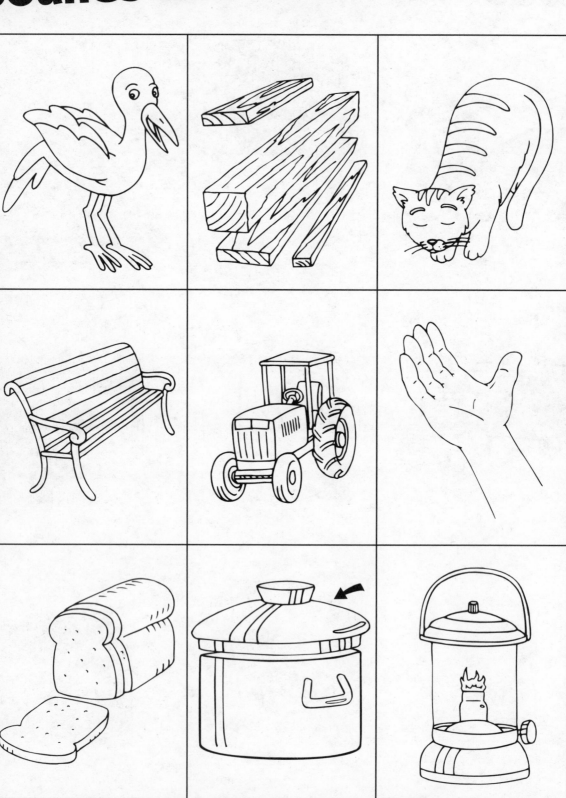

Sounds and Letters • Challenge

Name _____   Date _____

UNIT 4   The Wind • **Lesson 9** *What Happens When Wind Blows?*

▶ Sounds and Letters

Directions: Draw a line connecting the pictures whose names end with the same sound.

___d

___s

___m

 ___d

___s

 ___m

Copyright © SRA/McGraw-Hill. Permission is granted to reproduce this page for classroom use.

SOUNDS AND LETTERS

Challenge • *Sounds and Letters*   **UNIT 4 • Lesson 9   43**

▶Sounds and Letters

Directions: Circle each picture whose name begins with /p/.

SOUNDS AND LETTERS

▶ Matching Sounds and Letters

P p

SOUNDS AND LETTERS

UNIT 4 The Wind • **Lesson 11** *The Wind*

▶ Words That Show Action

Directions: Listen as I read the words that show action. Draw a line from the word to the picture of the action.

GRAMMAR AND USAGE

1. hug

2. sleep

3. jump

4. hang

Words That Show Action • **Challenge**

▶ Matching Sounds and Letters

SOUNDS AND LETTERS

▶ Matching Sounds and Letters

Directions: Find the word at the bottom of the page that names each picture. Write that word below the picture.

_____

- - - - - - - - - - - -

_____

_____

- - - - - - - - - - - -

_____

_____

- - - - - - - - - - - -

_____

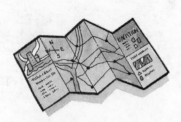

_____

- - - - - - - - - - - -

_____

_____

- - - - - - - - - - - -

_____

| pad | mad | sap | map | sad |

Matching Sounds and Letters • **Challenge**

UNIT 4 The Wind • **Lesson 14** *Fine Art*

▶ Matching Sounds and Letters

SOUNDS AND LETTERS

▶ Matching Sounds and Letters

SOUNDS AND LETTERS

▶Matching Sounds and Letters

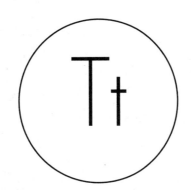

SOUNDS AND LETTERS

UNIT 4 The Wind • **Lesson 16** *Wind Says Good Night*

▶Review

Directions: Listen to the words I read. Draw a line from the word to the picture it matches.

GRAMMAR AND USAGE

1. soft

2. beside

3. eat

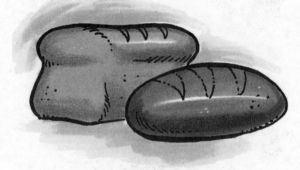

Review • Challenge

▶ Matching Sounds and Letters

Directions: Help the boy reach the bike shop by drawing a line connecting the pictures whose names have short /o/.

SOUNDS AND LETTERS

SOUNDS AND LETTERS

▶ Matching Sounds and Letters

Directions: Find the word at the bottom of the page that names each picture. Write that word below the picture.

Copyright © SRA/McGraw-Hill. Permission is granted to reproduce this page for classroom use.

_____

- - - - - - - - - - - - -

_____

_____

- - - - - - - - - - - - -

_____

_____

- - - - - - - - - - - - -

_____

_____

- - - - - - - - - - - - -

_____

_____

- - - - - - - - - - - - -

_____

dot   top   hot   mop   pot

▶ Matching Sounds and Letters

SOUNDS AND LETTERS

▶ Matching Sounds and Letters

SOUNDS AND LETTERS

Matching Sounds and Letters • Challenge

▶ Words That Show Action

1. We walk to the library.

2. He reads after dinner.

3. I ride my bike with my dad.

4. She looks for her coat.

5. They jump rope at recess.

6. We listen to the teacher.

GRAMMAR AND USAGE

UNIT 5 Stick to It • **Lesson 2** *The Great Big Enormous Turnip*

▶ # Sounds and Spelling

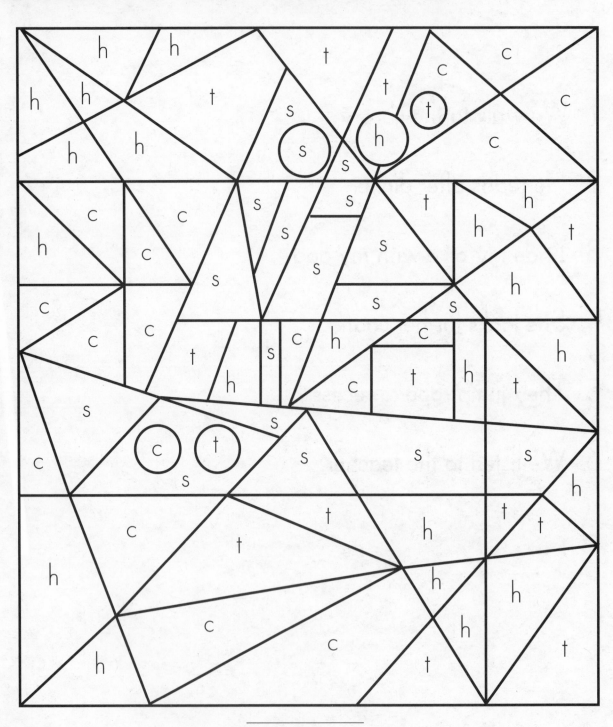

Sounds and Spelling • Challenge

UNIT 5 Stick to It • **Lesson 4** *The Great Big Enormous Turnip*

▶ Sounds and Spelling

SOUNDS AND LETTERS

_____

_ _ _ _ _

_____

WRITER'S CRAFT

▶ Current Events and Newspapers

Directions: Listen as I read the following list. Some things can be found in a newspaper, some things cannot. Put an X over the things that are not in a newspaper.

pictures

books

articles

names

apples

titles

stories

crayons

Current Events and Newspapers • **Challenge**

UNIT 5 **Stick to It • Lesson 5** *The Great Big Enormous Turnip*

▶ Matching Sounds and Letters

Directions: Help the worm reach the apple by drawing a line connecting the pictures whose names begin with /a/.

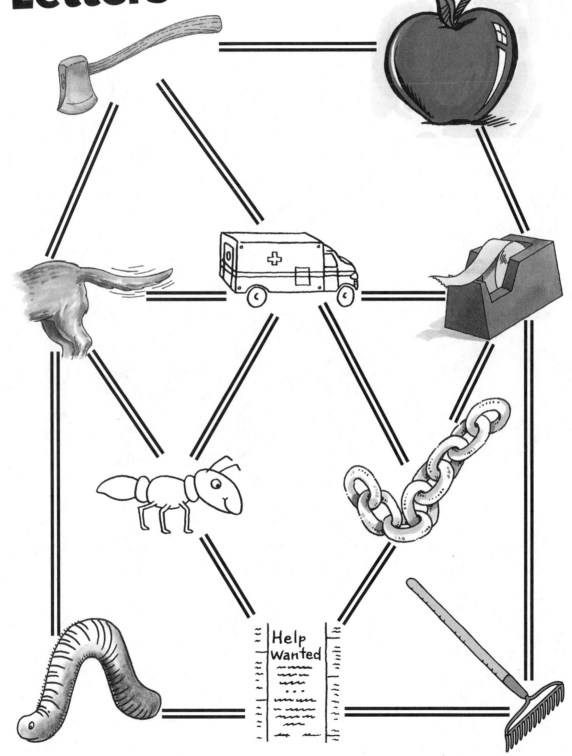

▶Matching Sounds and Letters

SOUNDS AND LETTERS

Matching Sounds and Letters • Challenge

►Words That Show Action: Tense, Present and Past

1. I paint pictures. He painted the fence.

2. She liked oranges. I like oranges.

3. The teacher smiles. The principal smiled.

4. They laugh. We laughed.

GRAMMAR AND USAGE

▶Sounds and Letters

Sounds and Letters • Challenge

UNIT 5 Stick to It • **Lesson 9** *Tillie and the Wall*

▶Time and Order Words

1. Today, I read a book.

2. Yesterday, we rode bikes.

3. Then, it was time for a nap.

4. Tomorrow, I will go to school.

WRITER'S CRAFT

GRAMMAR AND USAGE

▶ Words That Show Action: Past, Present, and Future Tenses

Directions: Listen as I read the sentences. Underline the sentence that uses the tense I read.

1. They ran. We will run.

2. She kicked the ball. He kicks the ball.

3. You will draw at home. We draw in class.

4. I will write you a letter. You wrote me first.

▶ Sounds and Spelling

Directions: Color each picture whose name begins with /h/. Then draw the path through the pictures to help the girl get home.

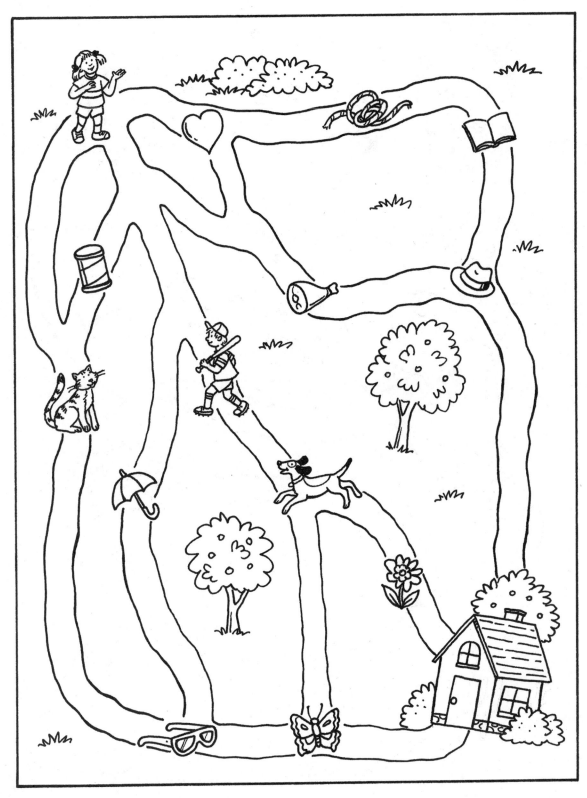

UNIT 5 Stick to It • **Lesson 13** *Fine Art*

▶Sounds and Spelling

Directions: Color the pictures whose names end with /p/. Then, draw the path connecting the pictures to help the boy find his cap.

SOUNDS AND LETTERS

Sounds and Spelling • **Challenge**

▶Sentence Elaboration

1. I went swimming.   at the beach   again

2. He likes to draw.   too   with crayons

3. She plays soccer.   also   at school

4. We talked.   on the phone   soon

WRITER'S CRAFT

▶ Sounds and Spelling

Directions: Circle each item whose name has /ī/.

SOUNDS AND LETTERS

Sounds and Spelling • **Challenge**

Review

1. We talked on the phone yesterday.

2. I will wear my favorite shirt.

3. I eat vegetable soup.

4. She will throw the ball to you.

GRAMMAR AND USAGE

▶ Sounds and Spelling

A•
B•
C•
D•
E• F• G• H• I• J•
K•
L•
M•
N•

Sounds and Spelling • **Challenge**

SOUNDS AND LETTERS

▶ Sounds and Spelling

Directions: Color the pictures whose names end with /l/.

SOUNDS AND LETTERS

▶Sounds and Spelling

Directions: Help the bird find its nest by following the path of pictures whose name begins with /n/.

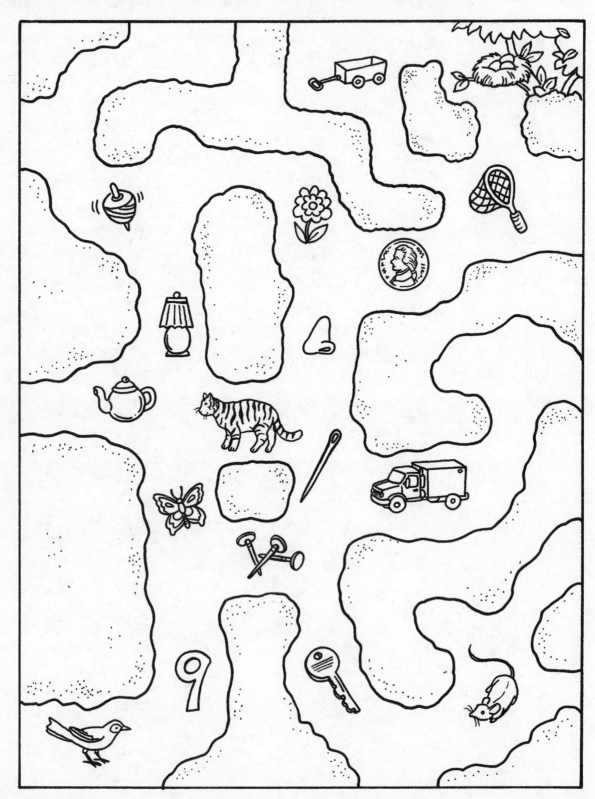

SOUNDS AND LETTERS

▶Capital Letters

1. dD _____ do you know William?

2. iI _____ She and i went to the store.

3. cC _____ How old is Aunt carol?

4. eE _____ elephants are gray.

MECHANICS

▶ Sounds and Spelling

SOUNDS AND LETTERS

Sounds and Spelling • **Challenge**

UNIT 6 Red, White, and Blue • **Lesson 4** *Patriotism*

▶Sounds and Letters

SOUNDS AND LETTERS

▶ Sounds and Spelling

SOUNDS AND LETTERS

Sounds and Spelling • **Challenge**

▶ Sentence Types

1. That's great   .   ?   !

2. Where do you live   .   ?   !

3. I live in Georgia   .   ?   !

4. You're the best   .   ?   !

GRAMMAR AND USAGE

▶Sounds and Letters

SOUNDS AND LETTERS

Directions: Draw a line connecting the letters *Bb* with each picture whose name begins with /b/.

Copyright © SRA/McGraw-Hill. Permission is granted to reproduce this page for classroom use.

Sounds and Letters • Challenge

▶ Sounds and Letters

Directions: Begin at the arrow and take the most direct route to the star by drawing a line that connects the pictures whose names end with /b/.

SOUNDS AND LETTERS

Location Words

Directions: Listen as I read each sentence. Circle the location word.

WRITER'S CRAFT

1. The cow is behind the barn.

2. The bird is above the tree.

3. The garage is between the road and the house.

4. The book is on the shelf.

5. The cat is under the bed.

6. The bread is in the oven.

▶ Sounds and Letters

Directions: Circle each picture whose name begins with /k/.

SOUNDS AND LETTERS

▶ End Marks

Directions: Listen as I read the sentences and the sentence type. Look at the end marks at the top of the page. Write the missing end mark to match the sentence type.

.	?	!

1. I enjoy reading _____

2. What do you read _____

3. I love books _____

▶Sounds and Spelling

SOUNDS AND LETTERS

▶ Sounds and Spelling

Directions: Draw a picture of something whose name ends with /r/. Then, write the letter *r* under the picture.

Copyright © SRA/McGraw-Hill. Permission is granted to reproduce this page for classroom use.

_____

_ _ _ _ _ _ _

_____

Sounds and Spelling • **Challenge**

▶Sensory Detail

Directions: Listen as I read each sentence. Circle the word that shows sensory detail.

1. The plate is too warm to hold.

2. The library is a quiet place.

3. My dog has soft fur.

4. The lemons are sour.

5. Is that your white shirt?

6. The brick is heavy.

WRITER'S CRAFT

▶Sounds and Letters

Directions: Help the frog hop to the pond. Circle only those rocks with pictures whose names have /u/.

Sounds and Letters • Challenge

▶Sounds and Spelling

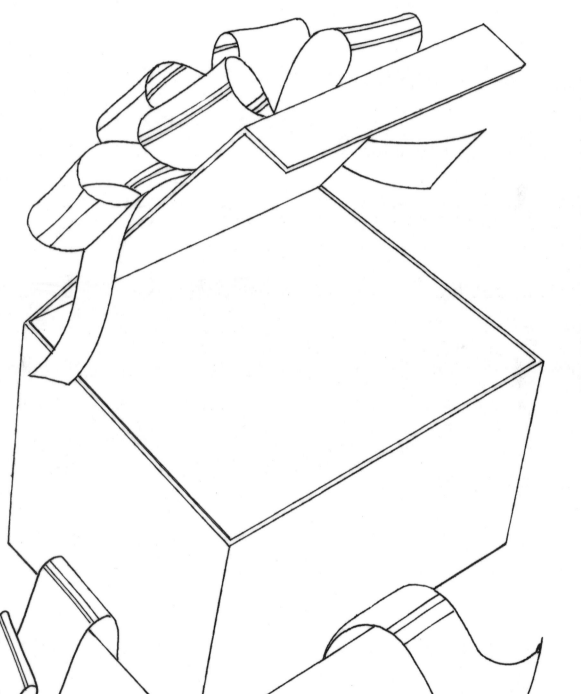

SOUNDS AND LETTERS

▶Review

GRAMMAR AND USAGE

Directions: Listen as I read each sentence. Underline the capital letters. Circle the end mark and the sentence type: S for statement, Q for question, and E for exclamation.

1. We love school!   S   Q   E

2. Do you know him?   S   Q   E

3. I brought my lunch.   S   Q   E

4. Good luck!   S   Q   E

▶Sounds and Spelling

Gg

SOUNDS AND LETTERS

_____

_ _ _ _ _ _ _ _ _ _ _ _ _ _ _ _ _ _

_____

UNIT 6 Red, White, and Blue • **Lesson 19** *The American Wei*

▶Sounds and Spelling

Directions: Draw a picture of something whose name begins with /j/. Then, write the letter *j* under the picture.

SOUNDS AND LETTERS

Sounds and Spelling • Challenge

UNIT 6 Red, White, and Blue • **Lesson 19** *The American Wei*

▶ Staying on Topic

1. The duck likes water. I am six years old. The duck is swimming.

2. It is raining today. Do you have an umbrella? I like apples.

3. My house is white and green. We went to the library. The library has my favorite books.

4. He plays the piano. She has a pet fish. He practices the piano after school.

WRITER'S CRAFT

►Sounds and Letters

Directions: Draw a line connecting the letters *Ff* with each picture whose name begins with /f/.

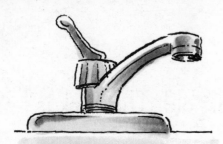

Ff

▶Pronouns: I and You

Directions: Listen as I read each sentence without the pronoun. Circle the pronoun *I* or *you* to complete the sentence.

1. [I/You] am sleeping.

2. [I/You] were at home.

3. [I/You] were jogging.

4. [I/You] am making lunch.

GRAMMAR AND USAGE

UNIT 7 Teamwork • **Lesson 2** *Teamwork*

▶Sounds and Spelling

SOUNDS AND LETTERS

Sounds and Spelling • Challenge

UNIT 7 Teamwork • **Lesson 4** *Teamwork*

▶Sounds and Letters

Directions: Draw a line connecting the picture in the center with each picture whose name has the same /e/ sound.

SOUNDS AND LETTERS

UNIT 7 Teamwork • **Lesson 5** *Teamwork*

▶Sound of Language: End Rhyme

WRITER'S CRAFT

cat

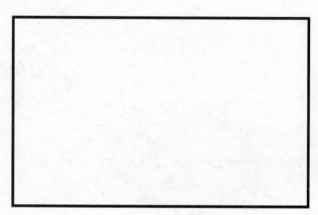

UNIT 7 Teamwork • **Lesson 6** *Swimmy*

▶Sounds and Letters

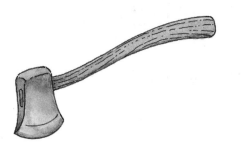

ax	box	fox	wax	mix

SOUNDS AND LETTERS

UNIT 7 Teamwork • **Lesson 6** *Swimmy*

▶Pronouns: He, She, It

GRAMMAR AND USAGE

1.

he   she   it

2.

he   she   it

3.

he   she   it

4.

he   she   it

Pronouns: He, She, It • **Challenge**

Name _____ Date _____

▶Sounds and Letters

Directions: Draw a picture of a zebra at the zoo and a buzzing bee.

SOUNDS AND LETTERS

▶ Sounds and Letters

SOUNDS AND LETTERS

_____

- - - - - - - - - - - - - - - -

_____

AH-CHOO!

_____

- - - - - - - - - - - - - - - -

_____

_____

- - - - - - - - - - - - - - - -

_____

_____

- - - - - - - - - - - - - - - -

_____

eyes	squeeze	sneeze	flows

Sounds and Letters • **Challenge**

UNIT 7 Teamwork • **Lesson 10** *Swimmy*

▶Sounds and Letters

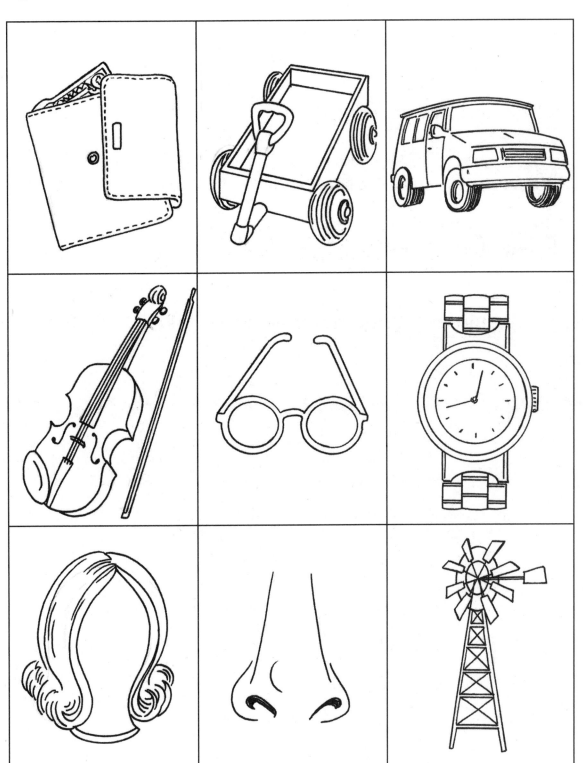

SOUNDS AND LETTERS

▶ Pronouns: We and They

Directions: Listen as I read each sentence. Circle the pronoun we or they to replace the underlined words in the sentence.

1. <u>Mark and Sonya</u> like to run.   We   They

2. <u>Mrs. Carter and I</u> write stories.   We   They

3. <u>Frank, Irene, and Sam</u> play ball.   We   They

4. <u>Grandma and I</u> ride horses.   We   They

GRAMMAR AND USAGE

▶Sounds and Spelling

Directions: Circle something in the first picture that starts with /k/. Then, draw a picture of something that begins with /k/ in the treasure chest.

SOUNDS AND LETTERS

Challenge • *Sounds and Spelling*

▶ Sounds and Letters

Directions: Help the duck reach the lake by following the path that connects the pictures whose names end with /k/.

SOUNDS AND LETTERS

Sounds and Letters • **Challenge**

UNIT 7 Teamwork • **Lesson 15** *Cleaning Up the Block*

▶Sounds and Spelling

SOUNDS AND LETTERS

▶Review

Directions: Listen as I read the story. Look at the story and the pronoun box carefully. Circle any pronouns you hear or see in the story.

| I | you | he | she | it | we | they |

My class went on a field trip. We went to the zoo. Jeff and Calley sat behind me. He is her brother. She and Jeff are my friends. I saw an elephant. It was drinking water. Have you been to the zoo? They were helpful at the zoo.

GRAMMAR AND USAGE

UNIT 7 Teamwork • **Lesson 17** *The Little Red Hen*

▶Sounds and Letters

Directions: Draw a line connecting the letters *Yy* with each picture whose name begins with /y/.

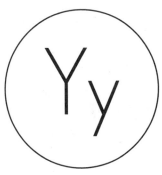

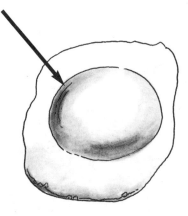

SOUNDS AND LETTERS

Challenge • *Sounds and Letters*

▶ Sounds and Letters

Directions: Draw a line connecting the letters *Vv* with each picture whose name begins or ends with /v/.

SOUNDS AND LETTERS

Sounds and Letters • Challenge

▶ Phonics Skills

SOUNDS AND LETTERS

_____
- - - - - - - - - - -
The _____ is sleeping.

_____
- - - - - - - - - - -
You need to _____ the batter.

_____
- - - - - - - - - - -
Does the _____ need water?

mix	plant	cat

Challenge • *Phonics Skills*

▶**Review**

teacher

horse

hat

park

Directions: Listen as I read each word that names. Draw a picture of the word that names in the box below it.

Review • **Challenge**

▶Phonics Skills

SOUNDS AND LETTERS

The _____ lives in water.

_____

- - - - - - - - - -

Is the _____ still there?

_____

- - - - - - - - - -

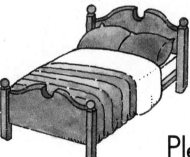

Please make your _____.

_____

- - - - - - - - - -

truck	clam	bed

► # Asking and Answering Questions

WRITER'S CRAFT

Directions: Listen as I read the questions and answers. Draw a line from the question to its answer.

1. What time is it?   My name is Tracie.

2. What is your name?   I am five years old.

3. How old are you?   I like elephants.

4. What is your favorite animal? It is 2:30 p.m.

▶Review

We swim at the beach. We build sandcastles at the beach. We play volleyball at the beach. We eat lunch at the beach. We walk and run on the beach. And, we sleep on the beach.

GRAMMAR AND USAGE

▶ Phonics Skills

_____

- - - - - - - - - -

I stepped on a _____.

_____

- - - - - - - - - -

Tom used a _____.

_____

- - - - - - - - - -

She found an _____ in the nest.

| hammer | egg | twig |

▶ Phonics Skills

Steve's _____ was white.

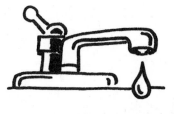

Did the sink _____?

The _____ needs to be cut.

| grass | drip | cuff |

SOUNDS AND LETTERS

▶Review

GRAMMAR AND USAGE

1. yellow

2. five

3. sunny

4. soft

5. on

▶Phonics Skills

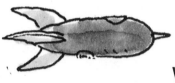

We saw the _____ take off.

Our new _____ was silver.

Did Ted lose his _____?

SOUNDS AND LETTERS

wallet	rocket	van

UNIT 8 By the Sea • **Lesson 14** *Fine Art*

▶Phonics Skills

SOUNDS AND LETTERS

_____

Let's _____ the car.

_____

Wendy dropped her _____.

_____

Was the _____ in the water?

| wax | duck | pen |

Phonics Skills • Challenge

▶Captions

_____

– – – – – – – – –

The _____ is empty.

▶Review

GRAMMAR, USAGE, AND MECHANICS

Directions: Listen as I read the story. Circle the capital letters and end marks you see. When you have finished, as a group, tell me the sentence type of what I read: *statement, question,* or *exclamation.*

I'm so excited! It's time for our family vacation.

Sometimes we go to Maine. This time we are going to

South Carolina. I can't wait! Have you ever been there?

We are going to have fun in South Carolina.

▶Phonics Skills

SOUNDS AND LETTERS

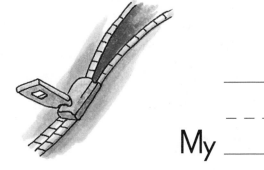

————
- - - - -
Dad used an _____ to cut the wood.

_____
- - - - - - - -
My _____ is stuck.

_____
- - - - - - - -
I like to wear my new _____.

watch	zipper	ax

▶ What Might Have Happened

Directions: Look at the picture. Draw a picture of what might have happened *before* the picture.

Copyright © SRA/McGraw-Hill. Permission is granted to reproduce this page for classroom use.